A NOTE TO PARENTS

When your children are ready to "step into reading," giving them the right books—and lots of them—is as crucial as giving them the right food to eat. **Step into Reading Books** present exciting stories and information reinforced with lively, colorful illustrations that make learning to read fun, satisfying, and worthwhile. They are priced so that acquiring an entire library of them is affordable. And they are beginning readers with an important difference—they're written on four levels.

Step 1 Books, with their very large type and extremely simple vocabulary, have been created for the very youngest readers. **Step 2 Books** are both longer and slightly more difficult. **Step 3 Books,** written to mid-second-grade reading levels, are for the child who has acquired even greater reading skills. **Step 4 Books** offer exciting nonfiction for the increasingly proficient reader.

Children develop at different ages. **Step into Reading Books,** with their four levels of reading, are designed to help children become good—and interested—readers *faster*. The grade levels assigned to the four steps—preschool through grade 1 for Step 1, grades 1 through 3 for Step 2, grades 2 and 3 for Step 3, and grades 2 through 4 for Step 4—are intended only as guides. Some children move through all four steps very rapidly; others climb the steps over a period of several years. These books will help your child "step into reading" in style!

To Caffery Garff–J.C.
To Ted–P.W.

Library of Congress Cataloging in Publication Data:
Cole, Joanna. Hungry, hungry sharks. (Step into reading. A Step 2 book) SUMMARY: A simple discussion of the kinds of sharks and their behavior. 1. Sharks—Juvenile literature.
[1. Sharks]   I. Wynne, Patricia, ill.   II. Title.   III. Series: Step into reading. Step 2 book.   QL638.9.C59   1986   597'.31   85-2218   ISBN: 0-394-87471-4 (trade); 0-394-97471-9 (lib. bdg.)

Manufactured in the United States of America

48   49   50

Step into Reading

HUNGRY, HUNGRY SHARKS

by Joanna Cole
illustrated by Patricia Wynne

A Step 2 Book

Random House New York

Millions and millions
of years ago,
the earth did not look
the way it does now.
Strange-looking plants
grew in swamps.
Reptiles with wings
flew in the air.

Everywhere on land were
dinosaurs, dinosaurs, dinosaurs.

Out at sea

there were strange creatures too.

Some looked like dragons.

Some looked like fish.

This big fish

could swim very fast.

It had sharp teeth

and a big fin on its back.

What kind of fish was this?

A shark!

There are no more
dinosaurs left on earth.
But there are still
plenty of sharks.

thresher

tiger shark

angel shark

10

Today there are more than
three hundred kinds of sharks.

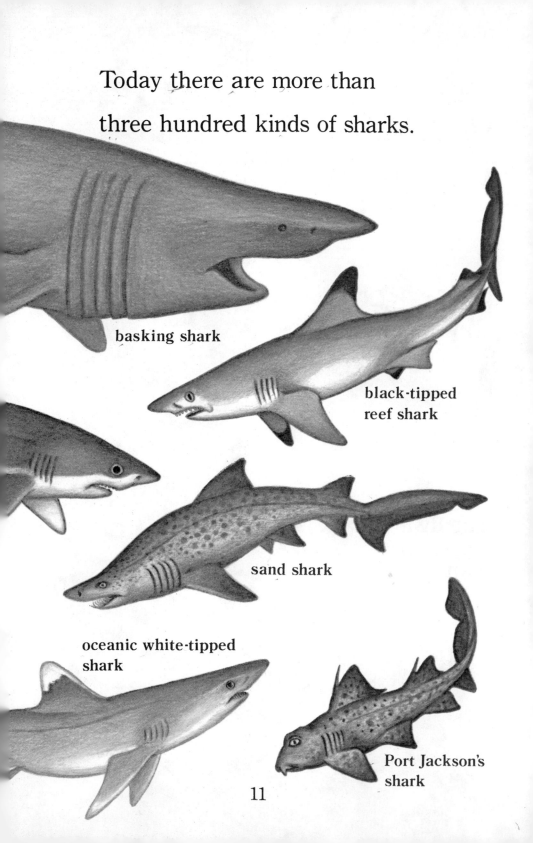

basking shark

black-tipped
reef shark

sand shark

oceanic white-tipped
shark

Port Jackson's
shark

11

Not all sharks are big.
Many, many kinds
are less than three feet long.

The dwarf shark is no bigger
than your hand.

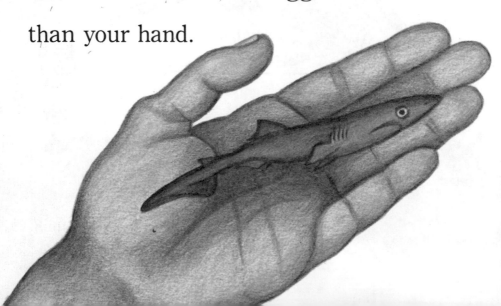

The small carpet shark lies

on the ocean floor

like a rug.

The leopard shark has spots.

It grows to be about four feet long.

The biggest shark
is the whale shark.
It is longer than a bus.
The whale shark
has three thousand teeth.
But it will never bite you.
It eats only tiny
shrimp and fish.

The whale shark is very gentle.
A diver can even hitch a ride
on its back.

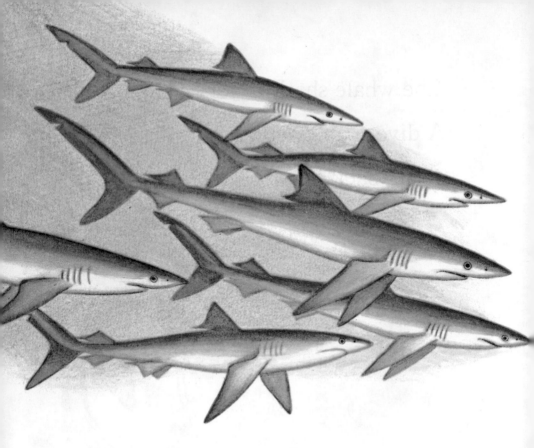

These are blue sharks.

They are far out at sea

hunting for food.

Suddenly

they pick up

the smell of blood.

The sharks speed up.

They shoot through the water

like torpedoes.

In a few minutes

they find a dead whale.

The blue sharks tear off
big chunks of whale meat.
Now the water is
full of biting sharks.

If one shark gets hurt,

the others turn on it.

They will eat that shark too.

In a short time

the whale is all gone.

The sharks swim away.

Nothing is left.

Nothing but bones.

Blue sharks are called

the wolves of the sea.

This is because

they stay together in packs.

Blue sharks often swim

after a ship for days.

A long time ago

sailors thought this meant that

someone was going to die.

Why do blue sharks
<u>really</u> follow ships?
The sharks come
because of noises
from the ship.
Then they stay to eat
garbage that is thrown
into the water.

The most dangerous shark

in the sea

is the great white shark.

It is named after

its white belly.

The teeth of the great white shark
are big and sharp.
Very, very sharp.
It can eat a whole seal
in one bite.
The great white shark is
the size of a speedboat.

This great white shark

has just had babies.

Most fish lay eggs.

But most sharks do not.

Their babies are born alive.

A baby shark is called a pup.

The pup of the great white shark

is almost the size of a man.

As soon as they are born

the pups go their own way.

It is not safe to stay

near a hungry mother.

The baby sharks swim off
to catch their own food.
One eats a fish.
Another gets a crab.
The pups had better
watch out for puffer fish.

The puffer fish can blow up
like a balloon.
If a shark eats it,
its spines get stuck
in the shark's throat.
The shark will die.

Not many animals

can kill great white sharks.

The stingray

flaps through the sea

like a giant bat.

Its tail has a poison stinger.

The poison can kill most animals.

But a great white shark

can eat a stingray—

stinger and all!

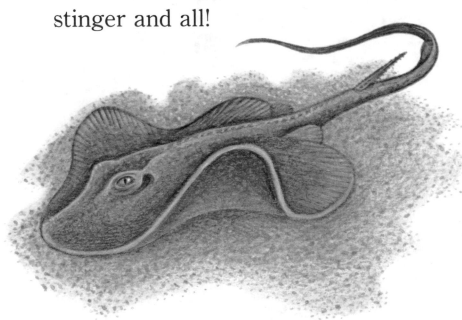

The swordfish is

a very strong fish.

It can cut and stab

with its long nose.

But even a swordfish

almost always loses a fight

with a great white shark.

Another big shark is

the hammerhead shark.

It is easy to see

how it got its name.

Like other big sharks,

the hammerhead never sleeps

and never stops swimming.

Most fish have air balloons

inside them.

But sharks do not.

If they stop swimming,

they sink.

This hammerhead swims
to a group of dolphins.
It tries to catch
one of the young dolphins.
But sharks do not always
get their way.
The dolphins fight back.

One dolphin dives

under the water.

It comes up and

hits the hammerhead.

The shark flies up

in the air.

It falls back on the water.

SMACK!

The dolphins keep
hitting the shark.
After a while
the shark stops moving.
It sinks down into the water.
It is dead.

Dolphins are smart animals.

They can work together

to kill an enemy.

But sharks are not as smart.

They have tiny brains.

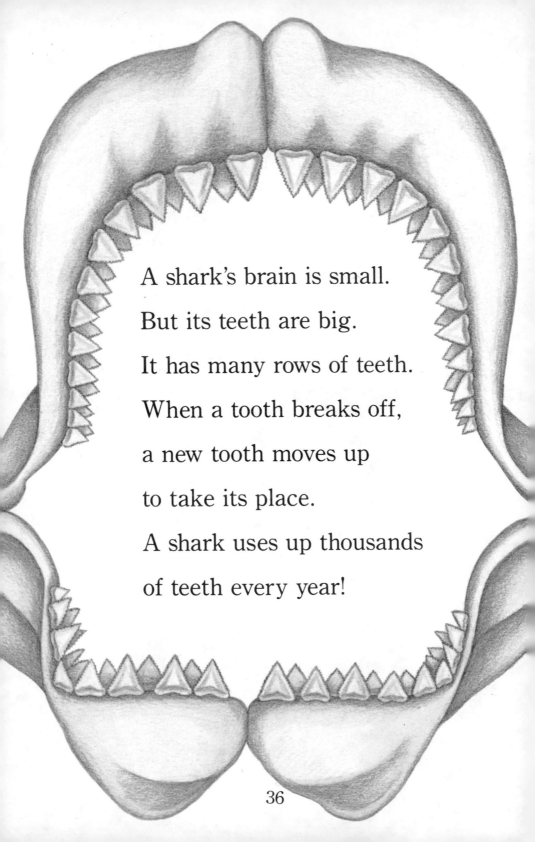

A shark's brain is small.

But its teeth are big.

It has many rows of teeth.

When a tooth breaks off,

a new tooth moves up

to take its place.

A shark uses up thousands

of teeth every year!

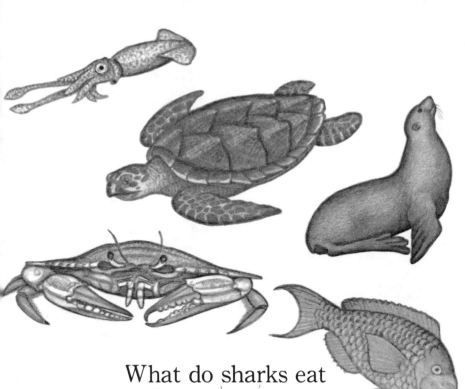

What do sharks eat
with all these teeth?
Fish and more fish.
Other sharks.
Seals,
turtles,
crabs.
Almost anything
that swims in the sea.

Sometimes sharks eat

things that are not food.

No one knows why.

All these things

have been found

inside big sharks:

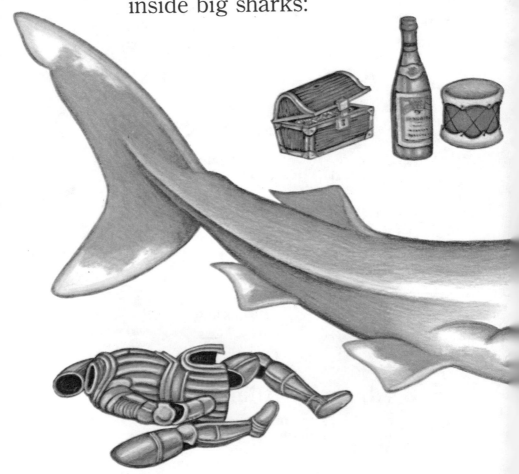

a wallet,

a fur coat,

a drum,

a bottle of wine,

a chest of jewels,

a barrel of nails,

and a suit of armor!

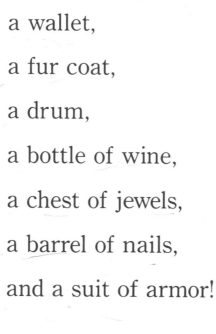

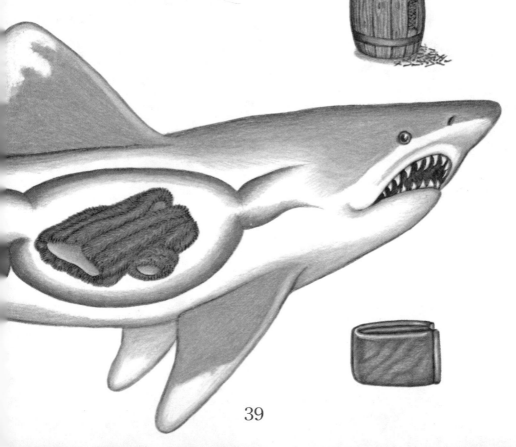

Do sharks eat people?

Yes, they do.

If a person is near a big shark,

the shark may attack.

Scientists want to study sharks.

But it is hard

to study them at sea.

And it is hard to keep

big sharks alive in a tank.

Once scientists caught

a great white shark.

They put it in a tank

with other fish.

But the shark did not eat.

And it kept bumping into

the sides of the tank.

After a few days

the shark began to die.

So the scientists

took the shark back to sea.

They set it free.

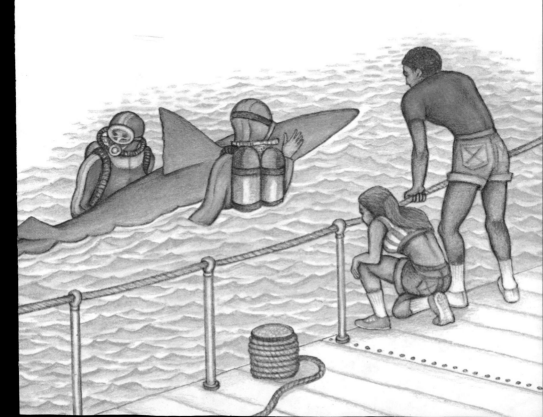

There are many things

we do not know about sharks.

We do not know

how long sharks live.

Or how much food

a shark has to eat

to stay alive.

But we do know that sharks

are here to stay.

They are fast and strong.

They hardly ever get sick.

And there is always

plenty of food for them.

As long as there are oceans,

there will be sharks.